Pat's Class Trip

by Jessica Evans
illustrated by Meryl Henderson

Core Decodable 25

Mc Graw Hill Education

Bothell, WA • Chicago, IL • Columbus, OH • New York, NY

MHEonline.com

Send all inquiries to:
McGraw-Hill Education
8787 Orion Place
Columbus, OH 43240

ISBN: 978-0-02-145519-5
MHID: 0-02-145519-8

Printed in the United States of America.

9 10 11 12 KOD 24

Pat's class was on a trip.

It was hot in the sand.

What did Pat's class miss?

What can hiss?

What can hop past?

What ran fast?

A rat did pass Pat's class.

Pat's class was back.

Pat's class trip was a blast!